NOT-FOR-PARENTS

CHINA
Everything you ever wanted to know

Scott Forbes

CONTENTS

HANDS UP IF YOU'RE LOOKING FORWARD TO THIS!

GOT ROOM FOR ME IN YOUR LUGGAGE?

'SNO JOKE VISITING IN WINTER!

LET'S TAKE IT FROM THE TOP!

IT ALL LOOKS GOOD FROM UP HERE!

COME ON DOWN! ANOTHER WORLD AWAITS...

REMEMBER: ALWAYS TRAVEL LIGHT!

I GOT IT ALL GOING, YOU KNOW. SO YOU CAN START BY THANKING ME!

NOT-FOR-PARENTS

THIS IS NOT A GUIDEBOOK. And it is definitely Not-for-parents.

IT IS THE REAL, INSIDE STORY about
one of the world's most exciting countries—China.
In this book you'll hear fascinating tales about ancient empires,
martial arts, the discovery of gunpowder, and the first cup of **tea**.

Check out cool stories about **ice sculptures**, dust storms,
bloodthirsty warriors, and **dragons**. You'll find acrobats, **fighting
crickets**, futuristic buildings, and some seriously **weird snacks**.

This book shows you a **CHINA** your parents
probably don't even know about.

DESCENDANTS OF THE DRAGON

Flashing fearsome fangs and talons—they frown at you from rooftops, loom above you on walls, stare at you from doorways, and peer out of porcelain pots—dragons are everywhere in China. In the West they might be seen as evil beasts, but the Chinese believe they bring good luck—Chinese people even refer to themselves as the "descendants of the dragon." So don't be afraid: those scaly, scary-faced, sharp-clawed critters are there to help!

IT'S MY FLAMING BALL!

High five
Some dragons might appear to be waving—showing off their credentials more like! Emperors decreed that only imperial dragons should have five toes. Dragons associated with commoners and foreigners had to have fewer.

SEE: FIVE AND FIVE! THAT'S ER...EH, HANG ON, IS IT NINE?

Staying on side
Chinese farmers never want to fall foul of dragons, for dragon gods are said to control the seas and weather. A well-timed offering to the gods might just ensure a good harvest!

THE FANTASTIC FOUR

The azure dragon is one of four awesome mythical creatures associated with the seasons and stars. The other three are the fearsome white tiger, the splendid vermilion phoenix, and, er, the black tortoise.

High security
Place a dragon or two on a temple roof and demons won't darken the door. Or so the theory goes.

NO, IT'S MINE!

AW, HANG ON GUYS, WAIT FOR ME!

HOW LONG IS THIS RACE GOING TO DRAG ON?

Getting ahead
Did you know that racing dragons is a 2,000-year-old pastime? Admittedly they're in the form of wooden boats with carved dragon-head prows. Just as well dragons are said to like water!

COME ON, SLOW COACH!

How to train a dragon?
The best way is to assemble a team of 30 to 50 people then make a wood-and-fabric dragon up to 230ft (70m) long. Hold it aloft on long poles and coordinate your movements so the dragon seems to move naturally. Do it well and you might end up performing at New Year festivals.

WANT MORE?

Dragon myths ✶ http://traditions.cultural-china.com/en/212Traditions1324.html

ONE AT A TIME, PLEASE!

Let's hope you're a people person because China is one packed place. It has the world's biggest population (1.3 billion) and is home to nearly one in five of all the people on Earth. In 1978, the government decided that the country was getting so crowded that from then on each family could have only one child. That slowed population growth, but more than 300 million babies have been born since— as many people as live in the entire United States!

OI! WAKE UP AND MOVE ALONG. MORE COMING THROUGH!

About 50,000 babies are born in China every day--roughly 35 a minute.

Saltwater sardines
Fancy a quiet swim? Well, you'd best avoid this saltwater swimming pool in the city of Suining in Sichuan Province. Up to 10,000 people pack the pool every day in summer and more than one million take a dip here each year.

WORLD POPULATION

CHINA 19.3%

REST OF WORLD 58.9%

INDIA 17%

USA 4.8%

IS MY RUBBER DUCK DOWN THERE?

GETTING AWAY FROM IT ALL

If you want room to move, head west, where huge areas have few or even no people. Of course, that's mainly because they are freezing cold mountains and scorching, sandy wastelands like the Gobi Desert. Not exactly inviting!

AH, PEACE AT LAST! NOW WHERE DID I PUT MY WATER BOTTLE?

GET OUT OF MY WAY!

It's all about me!
Some people think the one-child policy has resulted in a generation of spoiled children with little idea of how to interact with others. The Chinese call these kids "little emperors" or "little empresses."

OKAY, I CAN SEE IT NOW. TURN RIGHT, DAD.

When push comes to shove
Personal space is at a premium in cities like Shanghai. Vast crowds throng the streets and you'll have to jostle for space—never mind a seat—on trains and buses.

WANT MORE?

Latest population figures ✯ www.chinatoday.com/data/china.population.htm

GAME ON!

Chess and checkers, dominoes and cards, yo-yos and shuttlecocks—in China there's always a game on somewhere. You'll see people playing in houses, streets and playgrounds, cafes, parks, and gardens. Many games date back hundreds of years and have been exported to other parts of the world. Some might be familiar, but others are like nothing you've ever seen before!

Shape shifting
You don't need to know any Chinese to play tangram. Simply use the pieces to make shapes including animals, buildings, and people.

> BRINGING THAT LITTLE STOOL WAS SUCH A CRAFTY MOVE!

> 4998, 4999... TIME TO CHANGE LEGS!

Chinese chess
First played around AD 700, *xianqi* is a strategy game similar to Western chess. The contest represents a battle between two armies, each trying to capture the opposing general.

On the tiles
Mahjong is like a card game played with tiles instead of cards. It became a craze in the West in the 1920s after it was introduced to the United States by Joseph Park Babcock.

Look, no hands!
Jianzi, or kick shuttlecock, dates back to the 5th century BC. Players have to keep the shuttlecock in the air using their feet and any other parts of their body—except their hands.

The popular Western game of Chinese chequers is not Chinese but was invented in Germany in 1892.

In a spin

A Chinese yo-yo consists of a pair of sticks joined by a long string, along which you whirl wooden disks. Skilled players wow spectators with dazzling tricks. In the West, the game is known as diabolo.

3, 2, 1... READY FOR LIFT-OFF!

Black and white

Go is the world's oldest board game, dating back at least 4,000 years. The aim is to surround your opponent's pieces with yours.

IN THE RED CORNER...

Since the Middle Ages, crickets have been bred to do battle. Urged on by spectators, two crickets push, jostle, and jab until one backs down. Champions change hands for big money.

OKAY, YOU HIT ME WITH A RIGHT, AND I'LL GO DOWN. LET'S GET THIS OVER WITH QUICKLY.

WANT MORE?

Learn how to play mahjong ☆ http://mahjong.uchicago.edu/home.shtml

KEEPING IT IN THE FAMILY

Confused by Ming and Qing? Unsure about Song and Han? You need to get to grips with the dynasties. Until 1911, China was governed by a series of ruling families, or dynasties, that each provided one or more emperors. Of course, some emperors were more successful—or meaner and madder!—than others, and there were periods of bloodshed and chaos between dynasties. But it went, more or less, like this…

All together now

The long-lasting Han Dynasty helped the Chinese start to feel like one big family. Today 91% of Chinese consider themselves Han people. And that makes them the biggest ethnic group on Earth!

Xia Dynasty, 2200–1700 BC → Shang Dynasty, 1600–1046 BC → Zhou Dynasty, 1046–256 BC → Qin Dynasty, 221–206 BC → Han Dynasty, 206 BC–220 AD → Jin Dynasty, AD 266–420

THE FIRST EMPEROR

The first ruler to unite China, Qin Shihuang was a tough taskmaster with little time for the opinions of others. He burned all historical records except his own and executed 460 scholars who had dared to criticize him.

NICE DAY? DID I SAY IT WAS A NICE DAY? DID I?

Qin on film

Among the many books and films based on Qin Shihuang and his dynasty is the 2002 movie *Hero*, starring martial arts expert Jet Li.

The one and only Wu

Initially a concubine, Wu Zetian won Tang emperor Gaozong's heart after disposing of her main female rivals by having them beaten, their hands and feet cut off and finally drowned in barrels of wine. In AD 690 she deposed her own son and became China's only female emperor.

LIKE TO GIVE ME A HAND?

LET'S SEE: 'THERE WAS A YOUNG MAN FROM BEIJING...'

Top marks

An impressive military leader, 18th-century Qing emperor Qianlong was also a star scholar. He oversaw the publication of a four-million-page compendium of knowledge and wrote more than 40,000 poems.

| Southern & Northern Dynasties, AD 420–581 | → | Sui Dynasty, AD 581–618 | → | Tang Dynasty, AD 618–907 | → | Song Dynasty, 960–1279 | → | Yuan Dynasty, 1279–1368 | → | Ming Dynasty, 1368–1644 | → | Qing Dynasty, 1644–1911 |

I'M A VERY ADVANCED FISH!

Last of all

Imagine being made emperor aged two. And then being told at six that your dynasty is over (you'd have a tantrum, wouldn't you?). That's what happened to Puyi, last emperor of China. Later he spent 10 years in prison before ending his life as an ordinary citizen.

ME? EMPEROR? GREAT, I LIKE PLAYING SOLDIERS!

During the Song Dynasty, China was the world's most advanced civilization.

WANT MORE?

Find out about the early days ☆ www.ancientchina.co.uk

LOOKS GOOD ON PAPER

It's one of the handiest inventions ever. You can carry things in it, write and draw on it, use it for wrapping gifts, even fashion airplanes out of it. Understandably, Europeans were pretty pleased with themselves when they worked out how to make paper in the 13th century. Little did they know that the Chinese had beaten them to it—by more than 1,000 years!

HMM, MIGHT TRY ADDING SOME OLD SOCKS NEXT TIME.

Secret recipe
About 2,000 years ago, Chinese scholars had to write on strips of bamboo and sheets of silk. Fortunately for them, in AD 105 a court official called Cai Lun created the first-ever paper, using mashed up mulberry bark, plant matter, old rags, and bits of fishing nets. Quite a concoction!

JUST A TRIM, PLEASE!

Jianzhi, the art of paper cutting, dates back to the 6th century.

Bottoms up

Paper is used to make traditional Chinese lanterns. The medium-sized red ones are known, for obvious reasons, as tomato lights. The smallest type is called a baby's bottom lantern.

Making their mark

The Chinese devised various methods of printing onto paper. The *Diamond Sutra*, a Buddhist text, is the world's oldest printed book, dating from AD 868.

FIT FOR AN EMPEROR

The first-ever reference to toilet paper comes from a 6th-century Chinese scholar who wrote that he dared not use pages printed with classical texts "for toilet purposes." By the late 1300s, huge quantities of toilet paper were being made in China, including special extra-large, perfumed sheets for the royal family.

AH, THAT'S THE SIZE I NEED!

Hey big spenders

In the 9th century, merchants got sick of hauling heavy bundles of coins around, so they wrote each other notes promising to pay up later. The idea caught on and in the 10th century the Song government issued the world's first paper money.

WANT MORE?

Have a go at paper cutting ✫ **http://papercutting.net**

HOW TO MAKE PEOPLE LOOK SMALL

As emperor you want your subjects to feel small and powerless and make yourself look big and godlike. One way to do that is build a humungous palace—and keep it all to yourself. Clearly this was Emperor Yongle's thinking when in 1406 he ordered the construction of the Forbidden City. It became the imperial residence for the next 500 years—and no one but the royal family, trusted advisers and nervous official visitors was ever allowed in.

9,986...DOES A CUPBOARD COUNT? ER, WHERE WAS I? AW, NO!

Plenty of room
Built by one million workers over 14 years, the Forbidden City has at least 800 buildings and 9,000 rooms—some say 9,999. Do you think anyone has ever counted them?

I'VE GOT MY EYE ON YOU!

Scary entrance
Imagine you're a humble scholar on your way to meet Yongle. You enter the palace via a huge gate guarded by fierce stone lions—no doubt already feeling that little bit smaller!

WHAT, IT EVEN HAS ITS OWN RIVER?!

All alone on a sea of stone
Once inside, you have to cross one of five marble bridges over the Golden Stream and hike across the vast Outer Court to the Supreme Harmony Gate. And then there's still a way to go!

POSITIVELY NO ENTRY!

I LIKE TO SPREAD MYSELF ABOUT.

Hall of Heavenly Purity
This was Yongle's bedroom, so no way would you have got near here! Later emperors used it as a reception hall.

'The Forbidden City's main courtyard can hold 100,000 people.

Top of the pile
Emperor Yongle was the third Ming ruler—and a really, really BIG guy.

The Imperial Garden
Forever out of bounds to all but royals, this was where the emperor liked to relax.

Seat of power
An energy-sapping trek across yet another huge courtyard leads to the Hall of Supreme Harmony, still China's biggest wooden building. Inside, the emperor occupies a colossal throne. By this time, you're quaking in your boots and probably too befuddled to speak or even remember why you're here. Oh dear.

WANT MORE?

The Forbidden City is now a museum ☆ www.dpm.org.cn

ALL THE TEA IN CHINA

A fine day in China, 2737 BC. Emperor Shennong is traveling through countryside. At a rest stop, his servants bring him his usual drink of boiled water. As he reaches for it, a puff of wind drops a few leaves into the cup. He watches the water turn brown then takes a sip. "Not bad," he thinks, "I might try this again." Almost 5,000 years on from this fabled first sip, China is the biggest producer of what is, after water, the world's most popular drink.

Black tea leaves

COFFEE FOR ME!

CAN'T WAIT FOR OUR TEA BREAK.

Beginning to brew
However it was discovered, tea was being consumed in China by 1000 BC, mainly for medicinal purposes or as food. Tea drinking was widespread by the 7th century AD.

TEAHOUSE ETIQUETTE

Visiting a teahouse is a great way to experience traditional Chinese culture. But remember:
- ☆ Use two hands to lift your cup.
- ☆ Don't ask for sugar or milk.
- ☆ Drink slowly and savor the flavor.
- ☆ Don't place the cup, lid, and saucer on the table separately, as this indicates you are unhappy with the service—unless you are, of course!

High tea
Shanghai's famous Huxinting Teahouse has hosted heads of state including US President, Bill Clinton, and Queen Elizabeth II of Britain.

Man or myth?
A legendary figure, Shennong may or may not have existed. Often depicted as a rather scary looking guy, he is said to have introduced farming to China, as well as 365 types of medicinal plant.

YUM, I THINK I'LL CALL THIS LICORICE.

Some wild tea trees in China are nearly 3,000 years old.

Bloomin' lovely!
Teas are also made from flowers and herbs. Flower teas are served in glass vessels so you can see the dried flower slowly "bloom" in the boiling water.

Don't try this at home
Pouring tea this way could get very messy!

I'LL BEND OVER BACKWARDS TO PLEASE MY CUSTOMERS.

WANT MORE?

Learn more about the history and spread of tea drinking ✭ www.tea.co.uk

ARE YOU A RAT?

Or perhaps a monkey, or a rooster? Not sure? Then you'd better consult the Chinese zodiac. In China, everyone is associated with 1 of 12 animals, depending on their year of birth. Each animal has certain characteristics, which are said to be passed on to the people born in that year. The zodiac also tells you which other animals you'll get along with and which you should avoid—so be sure to check out your friends and family, too.

> NO, REALLY, I'M A RABBIT!

RABBIT
Year of birth: 1963, 1975, 1987, 1999, 2011
Character: Kind, sensitive, affectionate
Compatible with: Pigs, dragons, goats
Steer clear of: Rats, tigers

> IT'S MY BIG YEAR, SO MAKE ME LOOK GORGEOUS.

TIGER
Year of birth: 1962, 1974, 1986, 1998, 2010
Character: Confident, brave, volatile
Compatible with: Dogs, horses, monkeys
Steer clear of: Goats, oxen

OX
Year of birth: 1961, 1973, 1985, 1997, 2009
Character: Loyal, independent, hardworking
Compatible with: Rats, roosters, snakes
Steer clear of: Tigers, horses

RAT
Year of birth: 1960, 1972, 1984, 1996, 2008
Character: Charming, curious, ambitious
Compatible with: Dragons, monkeys, oxen
Steer clear of: Horses, rabbits

> YEP, I'M AHEAD OF THE PACK, HEH, HEH...

A warm welcome
China marks the New Year with colorful festivities—these guys are celebrating the Year of the Dragon in 2012. The Chinese year starts in late January, so people born in January are linked to the previous year's animal.

Pole position
It's said that the Buddha held a race to decide the order of the animals in the zodiac, and the rat won by hitching a lift on the ox's back then leaping in front at the finish.

PIG
Year of birth: 1971, 1983, 1995, 2007
Character: Giving, noble, trusting
Compatible with: Goats, dragons, pigs
Steer clear of: Snakes

DRAGON

Year of birth: 1964, 1976, 1988, 2000, 2012

Character: Powerful, intelligent, fortunate

Compatible with: Rats, pigs, rabbits

Steer clear of: Dragons, oxen

SNAKE

Year of birth: 1965, 1977, 1989, 2001, 2013

Character: Thoughtful, careful, determined

Compatible with: Roosters, oxen

Steer clear of: Pigs, snakes

HORSE

Year of birth: 1966, 1978, 1990, 2002, 2014

Character: Energetic, independent, adventurous

Compatible with: Dogs, tigers, goats

Steer clear of: Rats, monkeys, oxen

GOAT

Year of birth: 1967, 1979, 1991, 2003

Character: Sincere, artistic, generous

Compatible with: Pigs, rabbits, horses

Steer clear of: Tigers, roosters, oxen

The Five Elements

In turn, each animal is also associated with what the Chinese call the Five Elements or life forces—wood, fire, earth, metal, and water. For example, 2004 was the year of the wood monkey. Together the 12 animals and 5 elements create a 60-year cycle.

Intelligent?

MONKEY

Year of birth: 1968, 1980, 1992, 2004

Character: Outgoing, fun-loving, intelligent

Compatible with: Rats, monkeys, dragons

Steer clear of: Horses

ROOSTER

Year of birth: 1969, 1981, 1993, 2005

Character: Quick-thinking, efficient, honest

Compatible with: Snakes, oxen, pigs

Steer clear of: Roosters, goats

DOG

Year of birth: 1970, 1982, 1994, 2006

Character: Faithful, careful, supportive

Compatible with: Horses, tigers, pigs

Steer clear of: Dragons

WANT MORE?

Check out precise calendar dates and more ✯ www.chinesezodiac.org

THE TERRIBLE TARTARS

In the early 1200s, they suddenly swept out of Central Asia and carved out one of the biggest empires the world has ever seen. Fearsome and ferocious, the Mongols destroyed everything in their path. Terrified Europeans called them "dog-faced Tartars"—meaning, essentially, devils from hell—while the Chinese referred to them as rootless savages. Barbarians they might have been, but soon they had most of Asia on its knees.

HAVE I GOT YOUR EAR?

Grisly Genghis
Founder of the Mongol Empire, Genghis Khan is a candidate for the title of "Baddest Man Ever." He and his troops razed city after city. Genghis liked to keep a tally of the dead by having his soldiers take an ear from each victim.

Turn and run
A favorite Mongol trick was to have a small group of horsemen ride out and taunt the enemy, then turn and run. Feeling pretty cocky, their opponents would follow, only to find themselves ambushed—and obliterated—by a giant Mongol force.

In 1241, the Mongols were about to conquer Europe, but their leader Ögödei died so they turned round and went home.

GOT WHAT IT TAKES?

Life as a Mongol warrior wasn't all a bag of booty, and you needed certain qualities and skills to survive.

HOW'S THIS? GRR!

Horsemanship
The Mongols practically lived in the saddle, riding for weeks on end and sleeping on the ground.

A scary face
Alarming scars, whether from battles or shaving, were essential. A hat made of dog skin topped off that terrifying "dog-faced" look.

China is ours!
The Mongols seized northern China in 1234. Under Genghis's grandson, Kublai Khan, they conquered the rest of the country and in 1279 founded the Yuan Dynasty.

ARE WE THERE YET?

The high life
In China, Kublai proceeded to live it up in fabulous palaces. He even went into battle in the equivalent of a luxury tank—a pavilion atop four armored elephants.

WANT MORE?

It's thought that the Mongols wiped out between 30 and 60 million people.

FLYING HIGH

Is that a bird? Is it a plane? Or is it…? Most likely it's a kite. Kites were first flown in China about 3,000 years ago and kite-flying remains a hugely popular pastime. At almost any time and almost anywhere—in city parks and squares, in open fields and on beaches—you're likely to see all kinds of colorful shapes soaring, swooping, and diving overhead. So watch out!

> CAREFUL, I'M PRETTY SHARP.

> CUT IT OUT!

First cut
In ancient China, kite fliers would glue pieces of glass and pottery onto their kite strings. Then they would launch their kites and duel to see who could cut the other's kite string first.

Going up!
When powerful, warm air currents are rising, a strong kite can lift a person. So-called man-lifting kites were being used in China by the 13th century, for checking weather conditions—and for fun!

> REMEMBER TO LET GO SON!

Sky train
Kite trains consist of numerous small kites joined by a cord. Some are more than 330ft (100m) long and include up to 200 small kites.

Early kite fliers attached pipes, whistles, and strings-- even miniature harps-- to kites so they would make a musical sound as they flew.

Light for flight
Even 3,000 years ago, China had ideal materials for making kites: light but strong bamboo canes and sheets of silk. From the 6th century onward, kites were also made with paper.

KITE CENTRAL

The city of Weifang in eastern China is regarded as the kite capital of the world. Each year in April it hosts a kite festival that attracts thousands of competitors and enthusiasts from around the globe.

COME ON, IT'S EASY, JUST FLAP YOUR WINGS!

WANT MORE?

Learn how to fly a kite ☆ **www.drachen.org/learn/kite-basics**

CITIFICATION!

China is booming and millions of people are hot-footing it from the country to the city to work in factories, offices, and stores—between 15 and 20 million of them every year! As a result, towering apartment blocks, massive housing developments and even entire new cities are sprouting all over the country at an incredible rate.

Mass exodus
In the old days most Chinese lived in rural areas—as recently as 1950 the countryside was home to almost 90 per cent of the population. Today more than half of all Chinese are city slickers.

WHERE DID EVERYONE GO?

More people live in the city of Shanghai than in the whole of Australia.

The changing face of China
Between 2005 and 2025, China's city-dwelling population is expected to grow by 350 million. That's more than all the citizens of the United States!

1950	11%	89%
2030	70%	30%

■ People living in cities   ■ People living in the country

LET'S HOPE THAT ELEVATOR KEEPS WORKING.

Not so fast!

Kangbashi, in the booming northern mining district of Ordos, is a high-tech city made to house a million workers. The only problem is hardly anyone wants to live there! So far, most of the region's people have chosen to stay put in their villages and Kangbashi remains a ghost town.

The high life

By 2030, more than one billion Chinese will call a city home. With land space limited, the only way for city housing is up!

HI-HO, HI-HO, IT'S OFF TO WORK WE GO!

On the move

Cities are swelled further by ranks of temporary migrant workers— around 200 million of them. During vacations, they throng railway stations heading to and from the country.

JUST PASSING THROUGH!

PICKING UP THE PACE

The rate of city growth in China is truly phenomenal. No other country can keep up. And who'd want to? The construction costs alone are colossal.

Building big

More than 50,000 new skyscrapers will be built in China by 2025—the equivalent of 10 New Yorks, covering an area the size of Switzerland.

Shanghai skyline

Million-people cities

China already has 170 cities with more than one million inhabitants and will have about 220 by 2025. Europe currently has 35 cities that big, the United States just 9.

China 170 cities

Europe 35 cities

USA 9 cities

WANT MORE?

From 1013 to 1127, Kaifeng was the world's biggest city, with a million people.

NEEDLES AND...
CUPS?

For thousands of years, the Chinese have been jabbing, scalding and pummeling each other—for the sake of their health. Having needles stuck into your skin or hot cups placed on your back might look uncomfortable, but doctors and patients alike swear that such treatments not only banish aches and illnesses but also improve your overall sense of wellbeing. So, step this way please…

Yin yang symbol

A prickly character
This guy must have been really sick! Actually, it was a stunt to promote the use of acupuncture, at the start of the 2008 Beijing Olympic Games.

Life lines
How's your *qi*? The Chinese believe we all have a life force, *qi*, that flows around the body along channels, or meridians. If these channels are blocked, the balance of opposing forces in the body—what the Chinese call *yin* and *yang*—is upset, and illness is the result.

DID I REALLY NEED ONE IN MY GUM?

On target
Unblocking channels most often involves acupuncture—inserting long, thin needles into particular points along your meridians known as pressure points or *men* gates. Just relax, you won't feel a thing!

AT LEAST THIS WAY YOU DON'T INHALE.

I FEEL GREAT!

Light my fire

Acupuncture not having the desired effect? Then you might try moxibustion—attaching burning leaves to the needles to heat them. Or ear candling—sticking lighted candles in your ears to draw out toxins.

DO YOU SMELL BURNING?

Press here

Vigorous massage can also help stimulate the meridians.

HOT CUPS

Another option is cupping. Air inside a glass or bamboo cup is warmed. Then when the cup is placed on the skin the air contracts, sucking up the flesh and forming a tight seal. It's said to improve blood flow. It can certainly leave you with some interesting skin patterns!

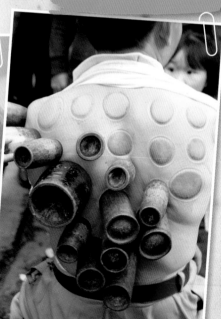

WANT MORE?

Brush up on the basics ✫ www.tcmworld.org/what_is_tcm

NOW YOU SEE IT...

Running right the way across China, it is, most definitely, the biggest human-made structure on Earth. But no one knows exactly how great the Great Wall of China really is. For it's not just one wall but many. Some date from as early as the 3rd century BC, while others were built in medieval times. And some run unbroken over vast distances, while others branch to dead ends, vanish under water or sand, or peter out in heaps of rubble.

Keep out!
China's first emperor, Qin Shihuang, created the Great Wall in the 3rd century BC to keep out warmongering nomads from the north. The Qin wall was made mainly of rammed earth and rocks and only small sections remain.

Bricks and mortar
From the late 1300s onward, the Ming rulers rebuilt and extended the wall using bricks and mortar. Long sections of this wall still stretch across fields and rollercoaster along ridges.

Wall of death
Qin Shihuang forced hundreds of thousands of people to work on the wall—up to one-fifth of the population—and thousands of them died on the job. In fact, so many people perished building the wall that it is sometimes called "the longest cemetery in the world."

I'M JUST ANOTHER BRICK IN THE WALL!

Building the wall may have cost the lives of up to two million people.

GLAD TO BE OF SERVICE!

A woof of smoke
As many as 10,000 watchtowers line the Great Wall. Soldiers used to burn huge piles of wolf dung and straw to send signals from one tower to the next.

Getting carried away
Over the centuries parts of the Great Wall have fallen into disrepair or even been carted away to build houses, stores, and roads.

Surprise! New sections of the Great Wall are regularly being found, usually in remote forest or desert.

...NOW YOU DON'T

A longstanding myth claims that the Great Wall is the only human-made structure visible from the Moon. However, the first moonwalkers said they couldn't see it. Nor could China's first astronaut, Yang Liwei, despite orbiting Earth 14 times in October 2003.

WALL? WHAT WALL?

WANT MORE?

The wall's length is at least the distance from San Francisco to New York and back.

IN CHARACTER

You might think it's tricky to master handwriting and spelling in English, but you only have 26 letters to deal with. Spare a thought for Chinese kids. Their language is made up of highly complicated symbols or characters, many thousands of which have to be learned before they can write well or read a book. No wonder some people call it the Great Wall of Chinese!

Far sighted

Legend has it that Chinese characters were invented around 2650 BC by the historian Cangjie. Looking at animal tracks in the sand, he realized that things could be represented by signs scratched into a surface. Cangjie was said to have four eyes, so perhaps it's not surprising he spotted this first!

Sun

Moon

Rain

Mountain

Fish

Cloud

Start simple

The first Chinese characters were probably pictographs—simple representations of the things they referred to.

There are now around 80,0000 Chinese characters, though many are seldom used.

Getting abstract

Gradually, combinations of pictographs came to stand for more abstract notions. For example, the characters for woman and child together make "good," *hao*.

Good =

好

Woman + child

From scratch

In 1899, a herbalist was grinding up bones to make medicine, when he spotted some symbols. It turned out the bone was 3,000 years old and carried the oldest Chinese writing ever found. Oops!

Hard graft
All you can do is practice,
practice, practice—there are no
shortcuts. By age nine, you need
to know about 2,000 characters.
Think you could handle it?

MIND YOUR LANGUAGE!

The characters make learning Chinese
hard enough, but for foreigners sounds
are an even bigger challenge. Different
pronunciations, or tones, can change
the meaning of a word entirely. For
example, saying *qing wen* one way
means "May I ask something?" But
change the tone a fraction and it
means "May I have a kiss?"

WANT
MORE?

Learn some basic phrases ☆ www.standardmandarin.com/chinesephrases

THE CHAIRMAN'S REVOLUTION

You'll see his face everywhere, watching from posters on buildings and adorning everything from stamps to bank notes. He's Mao Zedong, founder and first chairman of the People's Republic, and he's the man who transformed China. Not only did he introduce Communism, expand industry, and modernize agriculture, but he also fearlessly went head to head with the true enemy of the people: the sparrow.

TIMELINE

Mao cap

1912 Fall of the last emperor

1921 Founding of Chinese Communist Party

1927 Civil war breaks out between Nationalists and Communists

1937 Nationalists and Communists unite to fight Japan

1945 Civil war resumes

1949 Founding of People's Republic of China

1958 Mao launches Great Leap Forward

1966 Mao starts Cultural Revolution

1976 Death of Mao

The big winner
From the 1920s, two forces fought for control of China: the Communists under Mao and the Nationalists. In 1949, Mao won out and proclaimed the People's Republic of China.

Public Enemy No. 1

CAREFUL, HE'S A BIG ONE!

WHERE?

Threat to the state
Determined to modernize China, Mao began the so-called Great Leap Forward. He insisted people start industries. He also told them they must get rid of sparrows, as they were eating China's grain. So people blasted, trapped, and poisoned those pesky little birds.

GOOD, NO SPARROWS ANYWHERE. BUT WHAT'S THAT BUZZING SOUND?

Out with old ideas

Having dealt with sparrows, Mao moved on to teachers and other insufficiently revolutionary clever-clogs. He sent them to farms to learn how to work with their hands. This was called the Cultural Revolution. Not a good time to wear glasses.

DOWN WITH TEACHERS!

Waiting in the wings

But with every sparrow gone, locusts—which are usually eaten by sparrows—had a field day. They chomped through crops, adding hugely to the woes of farmers during a devastating famine in 1958–61.

UP CLOSE AND PERSONAL

Mao died in 1976, but you can still say hello to him. His embalmed body is displayed in a tomb in Tiananmen Square in Beijing.

More than a billion copies of Mao's Little Red Book have been printed.

Little red thoughts

You can also read his thoughts in his famous Little Red Book. It's essential reading for revolutionaries. No mention of those sparrows, though.

WANT MORE?

Mao never brushed his teeth, preferring to clean them with tea leaves.

TWO WHEELS TO GO

Across China, car ownership is on the rise and city streets are steadily filling with fume-belching, gas-guzzling vehicles. But, as they have done for decades, the vast majority of Chinese still depend on a much humbler and more eco-friendly form of transport, the bicycle.

ON YOUR BIKES, GET SET...GO!

Turning point
The bicycle took off in the 1950s when the Communist Party decided it was the ideal "people's vehicle." The main bike of that era, the Flying Pigeon, is the most popular vehicle in history, with more than 500 million sold.

Two-thirds of the world's bikes are made in China, including 9 out of 10 sold in the United States.

NOW, LET'S SEE: IT WAS GRAY, WITH TWO WHEELS...

Crazy foreigners
When Westerners first brought bicycles to China in the late 1800s, the locals thought they were mad. Wealthy Chinese preferred to pay someone to carry them in a sedan chair or rickshaw.

Survival skills
There are still around 500 million bicycles on the roads in China. To ride one in chaotic city traffic, you need nerves of steel–and a good memory!

MORE POWER TO THE PEOPLE

For the many Chinese who can't afford a car, motorized bikes–of all shapes and sizes—are the next best thing.

Live wires
Especially popular are eco-friendly electric bikes. More than 120 million of these now buzz around China's streets.

TURN RIGHT!

THESE NEW SELF-ASSEMBLY KITCHENS LOOK GREAT.

NO, LEFT!

All hands aboard
It's amazing what you—and a few friends—can do on a simple bicycle. Just don't try this in a Beijing bike jam!

Loaded up
Bikes are versatile vehicles. Add another wheel and you can transport almost anything— if you've got the legs for it.

WANT MORE?

About 90 per cent of all the electric bikes in the world are sold in China.

THE SECRET OF SILK

About 4,700 years ago, someone, somewhere in China, discovered something truly astonishing: that fiber from the cocoon of a particular moth could be woven into a marvelous material, called (in English) silk. Realizing the value of this discovery, the Chinese managed to keep the process secret for thousands of years—much to the fury of Western merchants, envoys, and emperors.

I STARTED IT ALL, YOU KNOW!

Silkworm moth

Mum's the word
As demand for silk grew, successive Chinese emperors decreed that anyone revealing the secret of its production to foreigners would be put to death.

Fancy fingerwork
If you wanted to make a robe like this one, you needed nimble fingers and infinite patience. Completing it could take up to eight years and six million stitches.

The ancient Romans adored silk, and valued it as highly as gold.

BY A THREAD

Psst, want to make silk? First, you'll need silkworms, the caterpillars of the Chinese silkworm moth.

Tuck in!
Start by feeding the worms with mulberry leaves, their favorite snack. This will help them grow to 70 times their original size.

Spit it out!
After a month each worm will form a long fiber with its saliva, and wind it around itself to make a cocoon.

Time to unwind…
Boil the fully formed cocoons to soften them and get rid of the pupae. Then unwind the fibre, which may be up to 0.6mi (1km) long. Finally, start weaving!

Beating a path
In the 2nd century BC, Chinese merchants took silk to Europe and Western merchants traveled to China along the so-called Silk Road. Yet still the source of silk remained a mystery in the West.

The secret is out
In the 5th century AD, Roman emperor Justinian persuaded two Persian monks living in China to smuggle silkworms to him inside hollow walking sticks. From those few worms, the entire European silk industry grew.

WANT MORE?

Travel the Silk Road ☆ http://idp.bl.uk/pages/education_students.a4d#3

HERE, HAVE A PANDA!

From the 1950s to the 1980s, any head of state visiting China was likely to go home with a hefty parting gift: a real live giant panda. The panda had come to represent the cute and cuddly face of China, so giving one to a passing president or prime minister seemed a great way to promote the nation. And it worked: in countries that received pandas, people flocked to zoos to see them, and they became national celebrities.

No Westerner saw a live panda until 1916, when German explorers purchased a cub in China.

Panda diplomacy
The Chinese practice of gifting pandas to foreign nations dates back hundreds of years, but it reached a peak in the late 20th century.

ZZZ

ER, UM... THANKS!

HOW MUCH CAN A PANDA BEAR?

Dwindling supplies
Handing out pandas seemed a rather rash thing to do given their rarity. By the late 1900s land clearance had confined pandas to tiny pockets of forest in the southwest. Even today there may be fewer than 1,600 in the wild, most living in protected reserves.

HOW WILL WE FIT THOSE IN OUR CASES?!

SURPRISE! SURPRISE!

MAYBE HE'D LIKE A CUP OF TEA?

Tit for tat

In 1972 the Chinese presented two pandas, Ling-Ling and Hsing-Hsing, to visiting US president, Richard Nixon. Nixon gave the pandas to the National Zoo in Washington, and later got his own by sending the Chinese two musk oxen.

HEH. JUST YOU WAIT!

Panda mania

A million people visited Ling-Ling and Hsing-Hsing in their first year at the National Zoo. Similar "panda mania" broke out in Britain when Prime Minister Edward Heath brought back Chia-Chia and Ching-Ching in 1974.

EATS SHOOTS AND LEAVES A MESS

Think you'd like a pet panda? Well, think again. It might look cute as a baby but a panda can grow to 6ft (1.8m) tall and weigh 350lb (160kg). Quite a handful!

Fussy eater

What's more, a panda requires an endless supply of bamboo shoots—up to 30lb (14kg) a day—and will eat almost nothing else. Oh, and a panda poops constantly, as often as 40 times a day. Still want one?

WANT MORE?

Learn how to help pandas ☆ http://pandasinternational.org

IF YOU CAN'T STAND THE HEAT...

At the height of summer, the average temperature in Beijing is 91°F (33°C), but it often soars as high as 104°F (40°C).

Located far from the cooling influence of the sea, China's capital, Beijing, swelters in summer heat. Ordinary folks have always had to just wipe their brows and tough it out. But if you were an emperor you'd find ways to stay cool. Even if it meant moving mountains. Or telling a few fibs.

Needing a change of scene
In 1750, Emperor Qianlong was fed up with baking in Beijing. He longed for shady, forested hillsides and wide, cooling waterways. Nowhere around the capital fitted that description. But was that a problem for an emperor? No way!

I WISH I COULD WEAR SHORTS!

Dig it?
Qianlong simply had 10,000 workers spend the next 14 years digging out a huge artificial lake, Kunming Lake, and using the earth to make a small mountain, Longevity Hill. Done!

Air conditioning
Once he had his water and hills, Qianlong planted gardens and built airy palaces and pavilions. He called his new hang-out the Garden of Clear Ripples, though it's better known now as the Summer Palace.

EVERY MOM SHOULD HAVE ONE!

PULLING THE STRINGS

Crafty Cixi was the real power behind the throne from 1856 to 1908, manipulating her husband, Emperor Xianfeng, her son, Emperor Tongzhi, and several successors. When officials visited her husband at the Summer Palace, Cixi would whisper instructions to him from behind a screen.

SHOULD BE GOOD ENOUGH TO FOOL THOSE IMPERIAL BEAN-COUNTERS!

The world's biggest sunshade

So that he and his mom could stroll along the lakeshore while staying out of the sun, Qianlong built a covered walkway, the longest structure of its type in the world, at 2,277ft (728m). He also had it decorated with over 8,000 exquisite artworks. Such a kind boy!

All aboard the HMS Cixi

In the late 1800s, Empress Cixi rebuilt the Summer Palace, using money she had requested to set up a naval college. She did at least build a boat. Not that it sails, though: it's made of wood, painted to look like marble.

WANT MORE?

Cixi even had a theatre built, so she could watch opera without leaving the palace.

A HANDSOME RETURN

Two hundred years ago, it didn't have much going for it: a small, remote island, home to a few fisherfolk and occasionally raided by pirates. But Hong Kong was still a handy hideout for British merchants. After acquiring a 99-year lease on the island in 1898, the British turned it into one of the world's great trading centers. And when the lease was up, China was only too happy to take Hong Kong back.

S'ALL RIGHT FOR PILLAGING, BUT YOU WOULDN'T WANT TO LIVE THERE!

Location, location, location!
Situated off the south coast of China, Hong Kong Island had no fresh water or farmland. But it did have a sheltered harbor and lay on the major trade route between the Far East and Europe.

THE CHEEK OF IT: NOT WANTING OUR BUSINESS!

CAN WE COME IN?

Getting their way
The sly Brits were smuggling a drug called opium. When China tried to stop this in the mid-1800s, Britain went to war, twice, in the so-called Opium Wars. Victorious both times, Britain forced China to buy its unhealthy merchandise and hand over more territory.

City of refuge
With trade guaranteed, business boomed. At the same time, Hong Kong became a refuge for people fleeing wars and persecution. By 1861, there were 120,000 people living there; by 1941, 1.6 million.

Rising fast
After World War II, British companies built factories to take advantage of the large workforce, and banks set up shop to supply the funds. Profits soared, high-rises rose higher, and the population climbed to seven million by 2009.

THAT'S THE BEST INVESTMENT WE EVER MADE!

IT'S THE GREAT CHINESE TAKEAWAY.

Hong Kong is one of the world's most densely populated places.

Hand it back!
By the time Prince Charles officially handed Hong Kong back to Chinese President Jiang Zemin in 1997, it was a business center to rival London or New York. China got its island back—and then some!

WHAT'S THE CHINESE FOR TIGGER?

WHERE EAST MEETS WEST

Not surprisingly, Hong Kong remains an island of Western influence. It's still home to large numbers of foreign people and businesses. It even has China's first Disneyland— and you don't get much more Western than that!

WANT MORE?

Find out what to do in Hong Kong ☆ **www.discoverhongkong.com**

HONG'S NOT-SO-HEAVENLY KINGDOM

Can you name the deadliest war of all time? World War II is right. And the second worst? No, not World War I but, many say, the Taiping Rebellion. Never heard of it? You're not alone. For this mid-1800s peasant uprising, led by a crazed visionary determined to found a heavenly kingdom on Earth is not widely known—even though it left many millions dead and devastated China.

Come again?
It all started with an unsuccessful student, Hong Xiuquan. After encounters with Christian missionaries and a series of visions, he claimed he was the second son of god— Jesus's kid brother!

YEAH, REALLY, HE'S MY BRO'.

I'LL DO ANYTHING FOR A LOAF OF BREAD!

Whatever you say!
Hong set out to create a "heavenly kingdom of great peace" (*taiping tianguo* in Chinese) and began recruiting followers. These were tough times, of famine and harsh rule by the Qing emperor. Desperate people were ready to believe anything.

WAR BY NUMBERS

The numbers in this grisly scoreboard of the worst wars and their dead are hotly debated, but there's no doubt China has had a rough ride:

- ✯ World War II, 1939–45: 40–70 million dead
- ✯ Taiping Rebellion, China, 1851–64: 20–50 million dead
- ✯ An Lushan Rebellion, China, AD 755–763: 13–35 million dead
- ✯ Qing conquest, China, 1616–62: 25 million dead
- ✯ World War I, 1914–19: 15 million dead

Out of control

Hong assembled an army that won victory after victory over the Qing forces. By 1853, this "Taiping" army numbered half a million and had seized the city of Nanjing. Soon the war spread all over China.

I LIKE TO BLEND IN.

Losing it

In Nanjing, Hong proclaimed his "Taiping Heavenly Kingdom." But he soon lost his mind completely and locked himself away with his wives, leaving much of the running of the kingdom to his 13-year-old son. What a job!

YOU HANDLE IT, I'M BUSY!

No surrender

The Qing recruited renowned British officer Charles "Chinese" Gordon, and his "Ever-Victorious Army" helped drive the last Taiping back to Nanjing. There in 1864, Hong died and many thousands of Taiping committed suicide rather than surrender.

WANT MORE?

Read the story in detail ✯ www.taipingrebellion.com

NEVER MESS WITH A MONK

As they meditate silently, chant softly, or tend their gardens, the Shaolin monks of Mount Shaoshi near Luoyang might appear meek, shy, and retiring. But breach their peace or upset their harmonious order and you might suddenly find yourself spinning through the air on your way to a rather uncomfortable meeting with a stone pillar or temple floor. For the Shaolins are the legendary masters of Chinese martial arts, or kung fu.

Fight club

In the 7th century, the monks honed their fighting prowess to defend themselves against bandits. Early techniques involved the use of weapons, but by the 17th century the monks had developed a form of fighting using only their bare hands.

TOO MUCH SITTING AROUND. YOU BOYS NEED SOME EXERCISE!

Bodhidharma

Home of the brave

The Shaolin Monastery was founded in AD 495. It's said that in the 6th century the founder of Zen Buddhism, Bodhidharma, taught the monks a set of exercises which became Shaolinquan, the first martial art.

I'M JUST PRAYING I CAN GET OUT OF THIS POSITION.

Hard men
Monks rise every day at 5 a.m. to begin study and training. Many exercises focus on toughening the body to turn it into what the monks call an "iron shirt."

Get knotted
Shaolin trainees quickly learn a host of handy skills, including headsprings, punching holes in trees with their fingers, running up walls, and meditating in very tight spaces.

There are now more than 60 martial arts training schools beside the Shaolin Monastery.

KUNG FU? I CAN DO THAT STANDING ON MY HEAD.

KUNG FU FIGHTING

In Chinese the term *kung fu* simply means 'skill' and is used to refer to all arts. As well as Shaolinquan, the many forms of martial or fighting arts include:

✭ Eagle Claw, which specializes in gripping techniques
✭ Bajiquan, famous for its elbow strikes
✭ Changquan, noted for its spectacular acrobatic kicks
✭ Wing Chun, a southern form of close-range combat

Health kicks
Tai chi is a martial art that is widely practiced as a form of exercise.

Mini master
In the *Kung Fu Panda* movies, the character of Master Shifu is based on a Shaolin teacher.

WANT MORE?

The media-savvy Shaolin monks have a website ✭ www.shaolin.org.cn/EN

HE WROTE THE RULES

You'd hardly think that some thoughts cooked up 2,500 years ago by a poor wandering scholar almost no one wanted to employ would be much heeded in the modern world. But to a quite amazing extent, the ideas of ancient philosopher Confucius still guide how many Chinese live and conduct themselves today—at home, at work, and at school.

GUYS, CHILL OUT!

Say no to violence
Confucius was born in 551 BC, during the so-called Warring States era. Horrified by the violence, he urged people to turn to the idea of *ren*, meaning "kindness." But those warring warlords just didn't want to know.

Be loyal to your leader
Confucius died in poverty in 479 BC, but his followers collected his thoughts in a book called the *Analects*. One of its central ideas was that of loyalty–to your country and its ruler. Emperors quite liked that idea and started to listen up.

PEOPLE MUST RESPECT THEIR LEADER.

SOUNDS GOOD TO ME!

Study hard and you'll succeed
A Confucian idea that caught on big time was that government jobs should be open to all, and awarded on the basis of exams. The Imperial Examinations system lasted from the 7th to the 20th century and convinced countless generations that studying is A Good Thing. Got that?

Learn the rules
Even today, young children are taught to recite the writings of Confucius. Sometimes very loudly.

Chinese children still study hard, spending an average of nine hours a day at school.

WE'RE RIGHT BEHIND YOU...

Obey your parents
Almost as important as loyalty to a ruler, for Confucius, was respect for ancestors and family. Most modern Chinese still listen carefully to their parents and grandparents, and few will dare miss a family occasion.

RESPECT WISDOM!

No doubt Confucius would be delighted by the respect shown for his ideas in modern China. People flock to his family estate at Qufu, now the site of the Confucius Temple. Not that he ever lived there: the grand estate was set up by his descendants, the Kongs, after successive emperors rewarded them with wealth and titles.

WANT MORE?

Bone up on Confucius's thoughts ☆ www.confucius.org

AN ILL WIND

Spring: it's a word that conjures up images of flowers, blue skies, and lambs frolicking across lush green fields. But don't count on such idyllic conditions in China. For spring is when winds whip western desert sands high into the sky and eastward across the entire country, turning the air into a suffocating smog and coating every surface with a thick layer of orange dust.

Country wide
The sandstorm in this satellite photo is whirling over almost the whole of China. Imagine how many people are under that!

The sky is falling
Once the winds are strong enough, the sand starts flying. This storm is about to engulf the northwestern city of Golmud.

Storms dump over
1 million tons of
sand on Beijing
every year.

March of the dunes

Sandstorms have got worse recently due to desertification—land turning into desert as a result of temperature rises and the clearing of trees. Windblown sand dunes are advancing east and are now just 50mi (80km) from Beijing. Within 20 years they could engulf the capital.

WHAT'S WRONG WITH A LITTLE BIT OF SAND?

Toxic cocktail

Airborne sand combines with China's high levels of industrial pollution to create a dangerous mix of sand and toxic substances such as carbon monoxide, arsenic, lead, coal ash, and pesticides. Yuck!

China's dust storms can trigger heavier snowfalls in the western United States--a bonus for skiers at least!

All a bit hazy

The dust regularly shrouds the major cities of the east, swirling through streets and reducing visibility. Airports often have to close and flights are grounded.

HE'S NORMALLY VERY CHATTY.

Wrapping up

People have learned to cope with the dust. They stay at home or wear masks and old clothes.

WANT MORE?

Up to a quarter of Los Angeles' smog is thought to come from China.

THE OLDEST SHOW IN TOWN

It's an amazing spectacle: colorful, beautiful, magical. And, yes, it's a bit baffling. A 200-year-old form of theater, Chinese opera combines music, dance, martial arts, bizarre costumes, and a lot of weird make-up. But don't let that put you off. It's not to be missed, and there are ways to work out what's going on!

Listen up!
The music is played by a small orchestra of stringed, wind and percussion instruments. Pay attention to the percussion, which often alerts you to dramatic moments.

Pipa

IT'S A TRULY UPLIFTING EXPERIENCE!

WE ALL NEED A LEG-UP NOW AND AGAIN!

Performance booster
Sure, it's performed in Chinese, but often it's a local dialect so many of the Chinese don't understand it all either. That means translations are often displayed above the stage—sometimes in English, too. How helpful is that?

> REMEMBER:
> DAN IS NOT
> A MAN!

The famous four
There are really only four main roles (from left to right): Dan, the female lead; Sheng, the male lead; Jing, the supporting male; and Chou, the clown. All are usually recognizable.

Color code
Look closely at the actors' make-up and masks and remember: red stands for loyalty and courage; blue and green are worn by brave, hot-headed characters; yellow and white indicate shifty types; and black stands for wisdom and strength. Got it?

Check out the moves
Watch out for acrobatic moves and fiery tricks. These are always appreciated by the audience. Soon you'll be nodding approvingly too!

READ THE SIGNS
Stay alert and you'll see that some actions are represented by gestures. Waving a whip stands in for riding a horse, for example. Patting the cheeks tells you a character is crying. Stroking a beard means a character is thinking.

WANT MORE?

History at ☆ http://asianhistory.about.com/od/arthistoryinasia/a/BeijingOpera.htm

ONE BIG BUDDHA

What has ears as tall as a two-story house and toes the size of a small car? No, not a prehistoric elephant but Dà Fó, the Grand Buddha of Leshan, in Sichuan, central China. Standing a whopping 230ft (71m) tall, it's the biggest stone Buddha in the world!

DON'T YOU DARE TICKLE MY FEET!

In one ear
Those long-lobed ears are 23ft (7m) high. The earhole looks like a top spot for a bird's nest!

The great protector
Dà Fó stands where three rivers merge, creating dangerous currents. The statue was started in AD 713 by a monk called Haitong, who believed it would protect river travelers.

Top to toe
While working on the excavation, Haitong lived in a cave behind Dà Fó's head. After he died, teams of monks and craftsmen slaved for 90 years to complete the carving.

I WONDER IF HIS PARENTS WERE TALL.

Before

After

ON A GRAND SCALE

Soon after Buddhism reached China in the 1st century AD, monks began creating extraordinary giant images of their religion's founder.

Spruced up
Just like you, Dà Fó needs a good scrub now and again. In his case it's not just to make him presentable but also to prevent erosion of the stone.

> I'VE SAID TO HIM, YOU CAN'T JUST SLEEP ALL DAY...

Dà Fó's hair incorporates 1,021 coiled buns, each one a stone peg slotted into the head.

Buddha at rest
At Dazu in southwestern China, a 90ft (15m) Buddha lies on its side behind statues of the men who paid for the shrine's construction.

> OH NO – FORGOT MY PRAYER BOOK!

> WE THINK BIG!

Keep off!
It's said that 100 people could sit in a ring on just one of the giant statue's feet, and at one time they were a popular picnic spot. But nowadays signs warn against treading on Dà Fó's toes!

Up for it?
To reach the 4th-century shrines on Maiji Shan in northwestern China, you have to climb hundreds of rickety wooden stairs attached to the side of a sheer cliff. Those monks must have had a head for heights!

The Longmen Caves at Luoyang contain over 100,000 carvings of the Buddha.

MADE IN CHINA

Take a close look at your toys, computers, music players, and sports gear. Chances are you'll find a "Made in China" label on most of them. For China makes and exports to the rest of the world a staggering range of stuff. It's all down to the country's productive mix of cutting-edge technology, giant factories, and the world's biggest workforce.

Ready and willing

China has an almost endless supply of increasingly skilled workers. Not only that, they generally work for much lower pay than workers in the West.

"I'M A YANKIE-DOODLE DANDY..."

Ways to save

Low wages, plentiful factories, readily available technology—what's not to like for manufacturers? It's no wonder that many Western firms have been shifting their production to China. It's partly how they keep their prices low.

Millions of American flags are made in China.

Heading your way

All this has resulted in ever greater piles of stuff being shipped from China to almost every corner of the world—including yours!

It's a shoe-in

China makes almost three-quarters of all shoes sold in the United States—and around 70% of the world's umbrellas.

WELL...IT'S WHERE WE COME FROM!

The toy story
China produces 90% of the world's toys, including at least three-quarters of all those sold in America.

AND THERE'S MORE ON ITS WAY!

Chips with that?
Half of all notebook computers run on chips made in the city of Chengdu, which is the base for 1,400 technology companies.

ANOTHER SIX MILLION? NO PROBLEM!

Celling out
Out of 1.8 billion cell phones made annually, about 1 billion are made in China, mostly around the southern city of Shenzhen. Six thousand Shenzhen companies work in the industry.

ROLL UP, ROLL UP...
Malls are popping up all over China—not that people are always ready for them. Opened in 2005, New South China Mall, in Dongguan, is the world's biggest mall. But due to poor transport services and low local wages it remains almost empty of stores.

WANT MORE?

Factories in the east-coast town of Datang make nine billion socks every year.

GOING WITH THE GRAIN

Rice is the food that turned China upside down. In ancient times, the north was the happening place while the rice-growing south was a swampy backwater with few people. But from the 6th century, rice fields began yielding giant crops. By the 1400s the south was home to three-quarters of all Chinese, and still is. And not only is rice now China's biggest crop, it's the staple food of half the world's people!

Brown rice is simply white rice with its husk still on.

Food for thought
Ever wondered what rice really is? It's the dried seed of the rice plant. Wild rice was first gathered in China 11,000 years ago and rice was first farmed there around 7000 BC.

TIME FOR A BREAK, I THINK.

Quick turnaround
Some varieties of rice grow in just three months. Then all you need to do is drain the field, harvest the crop, separate the seed from the husk—and start over again. Three crops a year is the usual target—phew!

Mud, glorious mud
If you want to roll out a rice crop, you need to get down and dirty. Rice is grown in flooded beds called paddy fields, and bending down to plant the seedlings is back-breaking work.

ONE SLIP AND I'M IN THE SOUP.

Stepping up production
Cut flat terraces into hillsides and you can grow rice on even the steepest slopes. As long as you have good balance and a head for heights!

RECYCLED RICE

The Chinese have found a host of uses for rice. Among other things, it's turned into wine, flour, straw, paper, crackers, noodles, and dumplings.

Instead of "How are you?", Chinese people often greet each other with the phrase "Have you had your rice today?"

Rice flour was once used as face-whitening make-up. Talk about a pancake face!

ANYONE FOR TABLE TENNIS?

WELL, HAVE YOU?!

Sticky stuff
Early Chinese builders used mashed sticky rice as mortar for walls—including the Great Wall of China!

WANT MORE?

Rice dumplings

Rice around the world ☆ www.fao.org/rice2004/en/aboutrice.htm

A LITTLE CORNER OF...WHEREVER

After the Treaty of Nanjing of 1842 allowed foreigners to live in some Chinese cities for the first time, Shanghai, the east coast's major port, quickly became home to thousands of people from all over the world. Through the early 1900s, wealthy foreign settlers built grand recreations of the streets and buildings of their homelands—Britain, France, America, Russia, and more. Soon you could hardly tell *where* you were!

The Bund

The Paris of the East
Pavement cafes, croissants, chic boutiques—surely it's Paris? No, it's the French Concession, formerly home to Shanghai's French community, and still one of its most glamorous neighborhoods.

French Concession

JUST LIKE 'OME!

GOSH, I DIDN'T KNOW HORSES PLAYED CRICKET!

Gathering place
Europeans liked to meet to watch horse races at the city's Old Racecourse, which also had a cricket field.

Rule Britannia

Remove a few signs and it could almost be London. The riverfront Bund is still lined with British colonial-style buildings, built in the 1920s when Shanghai was the world's third largest financial center.

Nanking Road

ALL IT NEEDS IS A LITTLE RAIN AND FOG...

The New York of the West

By the 1920s, Shanghai had a wild, colorful nightlife that rivaled that of Jazz-Age New York. Oversized American cars prowled past brightly lit bars, movie theaters, nightclubs, and dance halls.

In 1932, Shanghai was the world's fifth largest city and home to **70,000** foreigners, or "Shanghailanders."

UNDERWORLD

Shanghai had American-style nightlife, and the gangsters to match. Two rival criminal groups, the Green Gang and the Red Gang, had long fought for control of Shanghai's illegal businesses.

I'M ALL EARS, HUANG.

Police assistance

By the 1920s, the Green Gang, led by Du Yuesheng, or "Big-eared Du," had won out. This was thanks to support from "Pockmarked Huang," another gangster—who also happened to be a police chief!

WANT MORE?

History, photos, maps, and more ☆ **www.virtualshanghai.net**

HOW COOL IS THAT?

Midwinter in northeastern China. It's −22°F (−30°C) in the city of Harbin—teeth-chatteringly cold. You'd think everyone would be indoors huddled round a fire, or heading south to warmer climes. But no, hordes of people are not only crazy enough to be outside, but they are also busy shaping snow and ice to make sculptures and massive scale-model buildings. The entire city is gearing up for what is undoubtedly China's coolest annual show!

Harbin's ice festival began in 1985 and now draws 800,000 visitors every year.

HE COULD REALLY DO WITH A HAT.

Night lights
By day they might be simply shades of white, but by night, thanks to crafty computer-controlled lighting, the ice and snow take on every color of the rainbow in amazing "ice-lantern" shows.

Snow show
Snowmen? Pah, that's child's play! At Harbin snow is rolled, piled, and shaped with astounding artistry to create huge monuments and astonishingly realistic giant figures. Not a carrot in sight.

The world comes to Harbin
Once you've got the hang of building with ice, the world's your oyster. Knock up another Great Wall of China, an Egyptian Sphinx, or a European cathedral? No problem.

Bright spark
Once upon a time an ice lantern was just a hollow bucket-shaped block of ice with a candle inside. Technology has clearly moved on!

On the slide
You have to keep your wits about you climbing all those crystal-clear stairs, but coming down you can take the weight off your feet and just let go!

GLAD I WORE THREE PAIRS OF THERMAL UNDERWEAR!

BONKERS BEARS?

Still not cool enough for you? Then how about joining Harbin's "polar bears?" These hardy water-lovers take the plunge into a pool hacked out of the frozen Songhua River. Seasoned splashers swear it improves blood circulation and makes them more alert. Well, you're hardly likely to doze off in there!

OH-OH. MY HANDS ARE STUCK FAST.

WANT MORE?

YOU CAN TAKE IT WITH YOU

In ancient China, death was not the end. People believed you moved on to another life. Not only that but you could even take stuff with you. For ordinary folk that meant a few favorite knickknacks, for nobles usually some fancier treasures. But for Qin Shihuang, First Emperor of China, it meant, literally, his entire world.

BETTER GET STARTED. THIS COULD TAKE A WHILE!

Thinking ahead

Qin Shihuang began planning what to take with him as soon as he became emperor, in 246 BC. And over the next 36 years, he had over 700,000 people build and furnish his tomb.

Taking no chances

Clearly Qin Shihuang suspected the afterlife might not be all peace and tranquility, as he decided to take along an entire army. Sure, the soldiers were made of clay, or terracotta, but there were 8,000 of them. And they had real weapons and chariots.

WE'RE READY FOR ANYTHING!

Qin's world

At the center of his tomb Qin placed a bronze palace—full size of course. Around it he had labourers dig trenches and fill them with liquid mercury to represent the seas and rivers of the Qin world. And he had the tomb ceiling painted to look like the stars.

Individual treatment
A stickler for detail, Qin made sure everything at least looked real. Each soldier was given different clothes and facial features.

COOL OUTFIT, HUH?

A HEADS-UP

A farmer digging for water in a field in 1974 must have got the shock of his life when he dug up a lifelike clay head. That was the find that led archaeologists to Qin's tomb. Yet still only a small area has been excavated and most of the site, including the main palace, awaits discovery.

Some clay soldiers were armed with crossbows primed to shoot anyone who entered the tomb.

You're coming too!
For company, Qin took along dozens of wives—they were buried alive near his body. Finally, Qin's successors rounded up all the craftsmen who knew the tomb's secrets and walled them inside too, before covering everything with a mound of earth 250ft (76m) tall.

QIN'S ARMY

☆ 8,000 soldiers
☆ 130 chariots
☆ 670 horses
☆ 10,000 weapons

I KNEW THIS JOB WOULD BE THE DEATH OF ME!

WANT MORE?

The entire tomb is thought to cover 20 sq miles (50 sq km).

A BIRD IN THE HAND

Fishing: it can be a bit slow, can't it? Chucking out a line or net and then just sitting there, hoping that a fish will bite the hook or swim into the trap. But crafty Chinese anglers have managed to avoid all that hanging around *and* get something else to do most of the work—a bird. Their method is called cormorant fishing, and you might like to give it a go.

Where it's at
To learn from the masters, head south to Guilin, a major center of cormorant fishing, where spectacular limestone towers line the Li River.

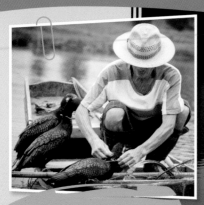

Tie a line
To keep the cormorant from swallowing all but the smallest fish, you have to tie a cord around its neck. That way bigger fish will stay in its throat.

BEST BETS

It's essential that you catch and tame the right kind of bird. In China, it's usually a great cormorant, though sometimes a darter is used; in Japan, the smaller Japanese cormorant is favored. Tie each line to the right species:

1. Great cormorant

2. Japanese cormorant

3. Rubber duck

4. Darter

a

b

c

d

Answers: 1=d; 2.=c; 3=b 4=a

Follow the light
Night time is the right time. Use a lamp to attract fish and light the way. Then pop the birds in the water and they'll paddle along beside the boat scooping up fish.

I'M A BIT SICK OF THIS!

Coming up!
A little bit of squeezing and tickling will persuade a bird to hand over its catch!

THEY'RE ENTIRELY THE WRONG KINDS OF BIRDS, YOU KNOW.

Smart anglers
The Chinese developed this nifty method more than 1,000 years ago.

THAT'S SEVEN. YOUR TURN TO COUGH UP!

KEEPING COUNT

Studies of cormorants have shown that the birds can actually count. Fishermen usually give them every eighth fish to eat. After they have handed over seven, the birds refuse to move until they are given their reward.

WANT MORE?

The Li River is one of China's most scenic areas ☆ www.visitguilin.org

TASTE TEST

China is a place for adventurous eaters. Not only can you tantalize your tastebuds with a totally scrumptious range of rice and noodle dishes, but you can also try out a host of delicacies and titbits you've almost certainly never sampled before. Feeling hungry—and brave?

AW...SO CUTE!

PEEKABOO!

As fresh as it gets

Seafood has got to be fresh, and live is as fresh as it gets. In China, you can not only select live sea creatures and have them quickly boiled or roasted, you can also eat them while they're still wriggling on your plate—octopus, shrimp, squid, crab, and more.

All you can eat

Long experience of famine and poverty has taught the Chinese to make the most of every food source. This means you can sample almost any meat you care (or don't care) to think of, including donkey, yak, and dog, as well as a huge range of plant roots, mosses, seaweeds, and insect larvae.

Many Chinese consider eating dairy foods such as butter and cheese to be quite disgusting.

ON THE MENU

Got a strong stomach? Think you can handle anything? Then take your pick from this menu of regional specialties.

APPETIZERS

Snake skin with peppers
Ducks' tongues
Shark's stomach soup
Boiled frog in radish soup
Dog-brain soup

ENTREES

Stir-fried camel foot
Simmered mountain rat with black beans
Whole pig face
Solidified duck blood
Cow's lung in chilli sauce
Spicy frogs' legs
Sliced donkey with noodles

DESSERTS

Insect cake
Red bean ice cream

A sticky business

In a hurry? Street vendors sell fast foods on sticks, including sparrows, silkworm chrysalises, cicadas, grasshoppers, starfish, and seahorses. Live scorpions are skewered and quickly roasted in hot oil—luckily that eliminates their sting!

Ducks' tongues

Whole pig face

Spit in your soup

Tiny swallow nests that the birds make with their saliva are considered a great delicacy in China. They are usually dished up as a soup, with the nest floating in broth.

WANT MORE?

Learn how to cook and eat Chinese food ☆ **http://chinesefood.about.com**

WHEN CHINA WENT TO SEA

Great sea voyages shaped our world–think of Columbus reaching the Americas–and they created global empires for nations such as Britain, Spain and, Portugal. China, though, could have beaten them all to it. In the early 1400s it had the world's biggest fleet of ships, which undertook several incredible journeys. Had those voyages continued, the world might be a very different place.

Traveling in style
Yongle had more than 1,600 ships decorated for Zheng He's voyages. And not just any old ships, but the biggest ones ever built.

Zheng He

COMING SOON, TO A PORT NEAR YOU!

Go west young man!
In 1405, Ming emperor Yongle commissioned Admiral Zheng He to lead the first of what would be seven voyages across the Indian Ocean to the West.

WHICH WAY IS UP?

The Chinese really got their bearings on the sea front by inventing the magnetic compass, which was first used during the 11th century.

Just add water
The earliest compasses consisted of a magnetized needle floating in water.

SO, ARE WE AT THE SHARP END?

AHOY THERE, MAKE WAY!

Portuguese caravel

Chinese treasure ship

DID YOU HEAR SOMETHING?

Call that a ship!
The fleet's flagships, the treasure ships, were between 400 and 500ft (120 and 150m) long—vastly bigger than a Portuguese ship of the period.

IT'S NICE TO SEE A BIT OF THE WORLD!

Zheng He's first fleet consisted of 317 ships, with a crew of 27,000-- including doctors, naturalists, and astrologers.

Well supplied
The treasure ships carried trade goods such as silk and porcelain, and massive supplies of food—they even grew vegetables on board! Souvenirs gathered by the fleet included a giraffe—the first to reach China.

Seen enough?
Over seven journeys, the fleet visited India, Arabia, and Africa. But then Yongle died. His successors decided the voyages were a waste of money, and cancelled further trips. China then turned inward once more.

WANT MORE?

Some think Zheng He also reached the Americas, but this remains unproven.

GODS AND MONSTERS

China's beginnings are a blur of history, religious beliefs, and fantastical legends. Powerful gods are said to have created the world, and the Chinese kingdom. Though the forces of darkness have often threatened to destroy these works, great heroes have usually been at hand to save the day.

YOU'D NEVER THINK CLOUDS WOULD BE SO HEAVY!

Giving his all

Some say it all started with Pangu, a huge hairy guy with two horns. He held up the sky for 18,000 years to separate it from the Earth. When he died, his eyes became the Sun and Moon, his hair the trees, his blood the rivers. Fleas on his body turned into animals and humans.

SORRY, FOLKS!

Top god

Others believe the world was begun by a group of gods led by the Jade Emperor. He is said to have made humans out of clay but then left them out in the rain, which is why we have disabilities and sicknesses. D'oh!

Demon

Devil

What a guy!

Legend has it that China was founded by the Yellow Emperor, Huangdi, who also introduced houses, carts, boats and writing and defeated the six-armed, four-eyed tyrant Chi You. These amazing feats are still celebrated on April 4 each year.

ALTOGETHER NOW: "FOR HE'S A JOLLY GOOD FELLOW..."

ROOM FOR ONE MORE? AND A DONKEY?

Super powers

The Eight Immortals are a group of legendary figures with super powers, who are said to fight evil, help people in distress, and restore peace. Some Chinese still worship them, and they have even featured in an X-Men comic book. Now that's immortality!

In 2006, DC Comics introduced a group of superheroes called The Great Ten, based on figures from Chinese myths.

Shape shifter

One of the most popular Chinese heroes is the Monkey King, Sun Wukong. Amazingly strong, he carries a staff that weighs 18,000lb (8,100kg), can somersault 33,500mi (54,000km), and can transform himself into 72 different creatures.

READY FOR SOME MONKEY BUSINESS?

Jet Li as the Monkey King, in the movie Forbidden Kingdom

WANT MORE?

Monkey King comic strip ★ www.china-on-site.com/monkey.php

LONG WAY TO THE TOP

One of the highest cities in the world, the ancient Tibetan capital of Lhasa, in western China, is a long way from anywhere. Traveling by road from Beijing takes several days via hair-raising mountain tracks and even China's speedy modern trains need three days to arrive. But if you're a devout Tibetan Buddhist, you'll be happy to take the hard way to this holy city—and walk.

An early start
Most Tibetan Buddhists plan to make the pilgrimage to Lhasa at some point, and some get a head start. Kids as young as five set off, sometimes leaving their parents for years and walking with other relatives.

Portable prayer wheel

Into thin air
Heading west, pilgrims climb into Tibet's high, cold, barren plateau. The air is so thin, it's hard to breathe. But at least the slow route allows you to acclimatize!

I'M TEMPTED TO JUST STAY HERE A WHILE.

Even harder yards
Trekking is tough enough, but if you're really serious you don't just walk. Every three steps you lie full out on the ground—an additional form of devotion called kowtowing.

NOW THIS IS FUN!

The end in sight
After such an epic trek, the sight of Lhasa could be overwhelming! Dominating the city is Potala Palace, the former home of Tibetan religious leader the Dalai Lama.

AT LAST!

Potala Palace has 1,000 rooms and houses 10,000 shrines and more than 200,000 holy statues.

Spinning around
In Lhasa, pilgrims walk twice-daily circuits of the holiest site, Jokhang Temple, turning prayer wheels—cylinders bearing religious texts.

I CHURN IT OUT!

HIGHER, HIGHER!
Some Buddhists take their devotion even further—and higher. Rongbuk Monastery is the highest monastery in the world and lies within sight of Mount Everest.

Buttering up
Pilgrims provide yak butter to keep holy candles alight.

Paying respects
And they make offerings, filling entire rooms with money.

WANT MORE?

Tibet is the world's highest place, with an average elevation of 16,000ft (4,900m).

BALANCING ACTS

Can you ride a unicycle? Juggle? Balance a tray of drinks on a stick on the end of your nose? And can you do all those things at the same time? Yes? Great! Then you could sign up for one of China's many acrobat schools. That's as long as you're still under eight years old and ready for ten years of grueling training. Sound okay?

Are you flexible?
The first thing you'll do at acrobat school is get your body into shape. Or rather, many really odd shapes. You might need a helping hand.

> ONCE THOSE LEGS POINT STRAIGHT UP, YOU'LL BE READY TO MOVE ON.

UP THERE WITH THE BEST

When you make it as a Chinese acrobat, you become part of a prestigious tradition that stretches back 2,000 years. Acrobats have been revered since the Han Dynasty (206 BC–AD 220) and often performed for emperors. Your family will be so proud!

Pick a trick
Maybe your specialty will be a brilliant balancing trick like this one. Just don't practice with your mum's best glassware.

Keep it up!
It's essential you learn to juggle just about anything— balls, sticks, plates, even tables. And not just with your hands. That would be too easy.

> THE DRINKS ARE ON ME!

WE'RE REALLY HOOKED ON THIS NOW!

Reaching your peak
Eventually, if all goes well (and there are no serious injuries), you might get to tour the world with a professional troupe, enjoying the excitement, the applause, and the lime light.

IN THE LINE-UP

Acrobatic performances are also known as Chinese variety art. Your repertoire will usually include the following:

☆ Conjuring ☆
☆ Contortionism ☆
☆ Plate spinning ☆
☆ Balancing glasses ☆
☆ Tightrope walking ☆
☆ Tumbling ☆
☆ Lion dance ☆
☆ Pole balancing ☆
☆ Hoop diving ☆
☆ Cycle tricks ☆
☆ Juggling ☆

WANT MORE?

China has about 120 acrobatic troupes and more than 12,000 performers.

A DROWNED WORLD

What if you had to move because the government wanted to build something where your home is? And not just you, but your whole village, town, or city. Hard to imagine, isn't it? But that's exactly what has happened to more than one million people living along central China's Yangtze River.

HOME, SWEET HOME!

Gorgeside living
The people were living along the Three Gorges. It's one of China's most scenic areas, so they probably thought they had it pretty good.

Water power
In 1994, the government started building a giant dam on the river, to harness its swift-flowing waters for power generation and prevent flooding downstream.

NO WAY AM I LEAVING IT BEHIND!

Moving on...or under
The dam raised the river level in the gorges by 330ft (100m). About 1.4 million people had to shift to new housing on higher ground—or start swimming!

YOU SHOULD SEE WHAT'S DOWN THERE!

Altogether the dam's waters have drowned:

13 cities, **140** towns, **1,350** villages, and **1,300** archeological sites

A watery grave?

Early people of the Yangtze placed their dead in coffins and perched them on sheer cliffs. Due to the raised river level, some now lie beneath the waters— while others can be viewed at closer quarters.

HEY, I CAN SEE MY HOUSE FROM HERE!

Window on the past

Hundreds of historic sites were swamped, including ancient stone carvings at Baiheliang. An underwater viewing room was built so people can still see them.

POWERING UP

Completed in 2006, the dam is not only one of the world's largest dams but also the biggest power-producing unit ever built. It will supply at least 3% of China's electricity, and protect 15 million people from flooding.

Turbines inside the dam

WANT MORE?

Dams are constantly being built in China—the country has 86,000 already!

WHAT I DID ON MY VACATION

Venice, Italy, 1271, and he's 17 years old. His dad asks if he fancies going on a business trip. Shouldn't take too long, says Dad. But somehow just getting there takes four *years*. And then they meet this old Khan guy and the next thing you know young Marco Polo is running all over his empire, for 17 years! Back home, Marco tells the story of his trip and—whaddya know?—it's a bestseller! And now it's all China, China, China!

ARE YOU SURE EAST IS THIS WAY?

Dad had a plan
Marco Polo's dad, Niccolò, and uncle, Maffeo, were successful merchants from Venice who had made one trip to China. It looked like they could do a roaring trade there, so they decided to go back—and took Marco with them.

We saw amazing things
On the way to China, wars and bandits made the Polos take many detours, and illnesses led to long stopovers. In 1275 they arrived at last and met Emperor Kublai Khan. They were astonished by his sumptuous palaces.

HOW ABOUT SOME PARMESAN? IT'S ALL THE RAGE IN ITALY!

GO AND TELL THEM THEY HAVE TO PAY MORE TAXES? ER, OKAY!

I went on a side trip
Kublai Khan made Marco a special ambassador and sent him to different parts of his empire.

MARCO? HE'S MY MAIN MAN!

Then I wrote it down

The Polos got home in 1295 – just in time for a war between Venice and Genoa. Jailed by the Genoese, Marco recounted his trip to cellmate and writer Rustichello da Pisa.

IT WAS SUNNY ...AND NICE.

HM, LET'S LIVEN IT UP A BIT, SHALL WE?

Marco's book inspired Columbus to seek a way to China--by going west across the Atlantic.

They can't get enough of it!

Published around 1300, Marco's book, *Il Milione*, was a sensation. It sent traders scurrying east, had people clamoring for Chinese goods such as spices and porcelain, and made people eager to learn more about the mysterious East.

Chinese porcelain

BUT DID HE REALLY GO?

Some people think Marco made it all up. He didn't mention tea or the Great Wall, and he said there were dog-faced people living in India. But most historians believe the account is true, just slightly eccentric!

DID YOU SEE THE CRAZY OUTFIT THAT ITALIAN GUY WAS WEARING?

TOTALLY WEIRD, MAN!

WANT MORE?

The Polos covered more than 15,000mi (24,000km) on their travels.

THE WRITE STUFF

Can you imagine your handwriting being framed and hung in a gallery? In China, the art of handwriting, or calligraphy, is universally appreciated and admired. A few deft strokes of a paintbrush can provoke nods of approval, gasps of amazement, and sighs of wonder. And a single written word or character might take pride of place in a museum or be sold for a fortune.

Forever *yong*
The eight basic strokes of calligraphy are all combined in the Chinese character *yong*, meaning "forever." Within any character, the eight strokes must be painted in a set order.

THE FOUR TREASURES

A traditional calligrapher works with paper, brush, ink stick, and ink stone. Together these tools are known as the Four Treasures of the Scholar.

Inky black
Made from soot and resin, the ink stick must be rubbed in water on an ink stone to create the ink.

HEY YOU, GET OFF MY ART!

Physical graffiti
Employing water instead of ink and paving stones in place of paper, artists regularly hold calligraphy competitions in Chinese parks. This pastime is also seen as a good way to keep fit.

So many ways to say...
This collector is displaying a set of 10,000 different handpainted characters, all representing the word "longevity" or "long life."

SAME OLD SAME OLD!

The art of calligraphy dates back at least 4,000 years.

THE PRICE IS RIGHT!

Highly prized
One of the most famous and revered calligraphers in history is Wang Xizhi, who lived during the 4th century. None of his original works survive, but copies do. In 2011 a medieval copy of one of his scrolls, consisting of just four lines of writing, sold for $46 million!

I GOT TOP MARKS.

GUESS I'D BETTER HOP TO IT!

Practice makes...clothes
Young children practise calligraphy from an early age. These school kids have created wacky costumes based on the character for "rabbit," to mark the Chinese Year of the Rabbit.

WANT MORE?

View masterworks ✫ www.chinaonlinemuseum.com/calligraphy-masters.php

CUTTING A DASH

Throughout history, China's rulers have set benchmarks for style with their swanky outfits and outlandish accessories. But although you might admire their sumptuous silks, groovy headgear, and wacky hairstyles, there are some Chinese fashions you'll be glad you missed out on.

AS LONG AS WE ALL FACE THE SAME WAY, WE'LL BE FINE.

YOU SHOULD SEE WHAT I'VE GOT UP THE OTHER SLEEVE!

Room to spare
For centuries, the height of fashion was a long silk robe tied at the waist with a belt. Fabulous patterns and rich colors, like those of this Tang-era robe, were a mark of wealth and privilege—as were gigantic sleeves.

Hazardous headwear
From the 2nd century BC, black hats were another status symbol. During the Song Dynasty, officials wore hats with two flaps that extended outwards from the head – as much as 3ft (1m). Imagine the injuries they must have caused!

Making a point
Long fingernails were a sign of wealth, as they indicated that you didn't have to do any work with your hands. This guy must have been loaded!

In the Ming era, women painted two tiny red petals on their lips to make a flower shape.

THE BIG SQUEEZE

From 1100 or so, it became fashionable for women to have really tiny tootsies, known as lotus feet. Getting just the right look involved binding a girl's feet tightly from an early age so that the toes curled under the sole and the arches bent upward, and usually broke. Ouch!

XXXSmall
The unfortunate women had no choice but to get used to tottering on their twisted stumps. Not until the 20th century was foot-binding banned.

IT'S THIS DYNASTY'S MUST-HAVE LOOK, SIR!

An orderly queue
When the Manchu founded the Qing Dynasty in 1644, they made everyone adopt their rather severe style—or face death! In particular, hair had to be shaved at the front and tied in a long pigtail, or queue, at the back.

OH DEAR, I'D BETTER CHECK THE CHAIRMAN'S MEASUREMENTS AGAIN!

Big in Beijing
After the 1912 revolution, wealthy women began wearing the elegant *cheongsam* dress. Men adopted the *zhongshan*, a military-style jacket and trousers. Later renamed the Mao suit after style guru Chairman Mao Zedong, it was very practical— as long as you got the right size.

Modern cheongsam dress

WANT MORE?

In the 1800s, roughly half of all Chinese women had bound feet.

FAST TRACK TO THE FUTURE

The face of China is changing at top speed.
Futuristic buildings are rapidly reshaping city skylines in
sci-fi style. Gargantuan railroads, bridges, and highways
are spanning seas and deserts. And superfast forms
of transport are whisking people here, there, and
everywhere, shrinking distances and
bringing the outside world that
big bit closer.

JUST HOPE
THEY'VE FINISHED
THE RUNWAY.

Between 2008
and 2020, China
plans to build 97
new airports!

ARE YOU SURE
WE'RE THE
RIGHT WAY UP?

Reaching for the sky

China now has almost half
of the world's top 20 highest
skyscrapers, including the
Shanghai Financial Center
(left) and Jin Mao Tower.

Visions realised

Famous architects are being
invited to let their imaginations
run riot and create ultramodern
buildings. Known to locals as
the Bird's Egg, Beijing's National
Center for the Performing Arts
was dreamed up by French
architect Paul Andreu.

Way to go

While relatively few Chinese (1 in 16) own a car, traffic jams are already a problem—one snarl-up in Beijing in 2010 stretched for 60mi (100km) and took nine days to clear. Imagine what it will be like if China matches the United States, where three out of every four people possess a car!

UH-OH, DID WE BRING ANY FOOD?

Bridging the gaps

Opened in 2011, the Jiaozhou Bridge is the world's longest over-sea bridge. Extending for 26.5mi (100km), it links the cities of Qingdao and Huangdo across Jiaozhou Bay and is designed to withstand earthquakes and typhoons.

AS SOON AS I PRESS THIS LITTLE BUTTON HERE, YOU'LL BE FLYING TO BEIJING.

SPEEDING UP

China introduced high-speed trains in 2007 and already has by far the world's longest high-speed network. Plans are afoot to connect it to Europe.

WILL THE TRAIN COME TOO?

Express delivery

Shanghai's Maglev train, which links the city to the airport, can operate at speeds of up to 267mph (430km/h).

City link

The Beijing–Shanghai High-Speed Railway covers the 819mi (1,318km) journey between the cities in less than five hours.

WANT MORE?

GOING OFF WITH A BANG

Imagine their astonishment. In the 9th century, Chinese monks searching for a substance that would grant eternal life whipped up a mix of sulfur, charcoal, and potassium nitrate (also called saltpeter). Touching it to a flame they found it not only burned brightly but instantly exploded—with a blast of hot gas and an ear-splitting bang. The monks didn't have much use for this "black powder" or "fire medicine," as they called it. But others—who later renamed it gunpowder—sure did!

COOL! WHAT CAN WE BLOW UP NEXT?

THESE MONKS ARE CRAZY!

Trial and error
Some monks reported that as a result of mixing "fire medicine" their hands and faces were scorched and the houses they were working in burned down. Oops!

Strike a light!

Not surprisingly, people at first kept their distance from the black powder, and it was used mainly for sending signals. But then some folks began to think the explosions were fun. And so fireworks were born.

Bombs away!

More warlike Chinese realized those bright, superhot blasts could be a handy weapon. In the 12th century, military leaders began making basic rockets, guns, and bombs.

HAVING A BLAST

Experiments proved it was precise proportions of the ingredients that created such a powerfully explosive mixture:

75% saltpeter +
15% charcoal +
10% sulfur
= BOOM!

Pulling the trigger

In the 13th century the Mongols seized on the new technology and used it against enemies in West Asia and Europe. Soon gunpowder weapons were everywhere. And the world was never the same again!

In the 10th century firecrackers were used to scare away evil spirits.

LET'S CALL IT...

Chinese names for early weapons were descriptive and colorful. Link the name to the right definition:

1. "Poison-fog magic smoke eruptor"

A. A grenade-like bomb attached to an arrow

2. "Flying-sand magic bomb releasing 10,000 fires"

B. A cannonball that released poisonous gas

3. "Mysteriously moving, infantry-breaking fierce-flame sword-shield"

C. An explosive pot filled with sand, sticky resin, and liquid from poisonous plants

4. "Fiery pomegranate shot from a bow"

D. A huge shield on wheels through which gunmen could fire

Answers: 1=B; 2=C; 3=D; 4=A.

WANT MORE?

Early weapons manual ☆ http://history.cultural-china.com/en/37History6314.html

GET LUCKY!

Things not working out the way you hoped? Worried about the future? In China it's thought that there are many ways to boost your fortunes, change things for the better, and pave the way to prosperity. It might mean redesigning your house or wearing the right clothes, or simply picking the right numbers—and avoiding the wrong ones!

Dress for success

Forget fashion—choose colors that bring you favor. Red is considered the luckiest color, and is seen everywhere at New Year. Yellow brings good luck too, but white is linked with mourning and therefore misfortune.

LUCKY THERE ARE SIX OF US!

Traditional lucky knot

DO THE NUMBERS

In China, numbers have either good or bad associations, often depending on the words they sound like in Chinese. Link yourself with lucky numbers and steer clear of the unlucky ones.

一 **1** Neutral

二 **2** Usually positive: associated with doubles and pairs

三 **3** Lucky: sounds like the word for "birth"

四 **4** Oh-oh, the worst number: sounds like "death"

五 **5** Neither lucky nor unlucky

六 **6** Lucky: sounds like "flow"

七 **7** Good for relationships, as it symbolizes togetherness

八 **8** Brings good fortune in business: sounds like "wealth"

九 **9** Lucky: linked with emperors and long life

88 CENTS – GEE, THANKS.

Pass it on
Want to pass on your good fortune? Give a friend some money in a lucky red envelope, or *hongbao*. Make sure the total sum includes an 8 or a 2—but please, no 4s!

Many Chinese buildings skip floor numbers containing the number 4. So there may be no level 4, 14 and so on--or any at all between 39 and 50!

Put your house in order
For help on the home front, consult a practitioner of feng shui. According to this ancient art, the arrangement of furniture and doorways is said to affect the flow of energy and enhance wellbeing.

Stick it up
The Chinese character *fu* means "luck." Stick one on your door—but upside down. That's because the words for "upside down" and "arrives" sound the same in Chinese. So that way "luck arrives"—hopefully!

WANT MORE?

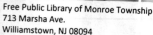

Free Public Library of Monroe Township
713 Marsha Ave.
Williamstown, NJ 08094

The fear of the number 4, which is common in Asia, is called tetraphobia.

INDEX

NOT-FOR-PARENTS
CHINA
EVERYTHING YOU EVER WANTED TO KNOW

1st Edition
Published September 2012

Conceived by Weldon Owen in partnership with Lonely Planet
Produced by Weldon Owen Publishing
Northburgh House, 10 Northburgh Street
London, EC1V 0AT, UK

weldonowenpublishing.com

Copyright © 2012 Weldon Owen Publishing

WELDONOWEN
PUBLISHING

WELDON OWEN LTD

Managing Director Sarah Odedina
Publisher Corinne Roberts
Creative Director Sue Burk
Sales Director Laurence Richard
Sales Manager, North America Ellen Towell
Designer Adam Walker
Design Assistant Haylee Bruce
Index Puddingburn Publishing Services
Production Director Dominic Saraceno
Production Controller Tristan Hanks

Published by
Lonely Planet Publications Pty Ltd ABN 36 005 607 983
90 Maribyrnong St, Footscray, Victoria 3011, Australia

ISBN 978-1-7432-1427-5

Printed in China

A WELDON OWEN PRODUCTION

Credits and acknowledgments

Key tl=top left; tcl=top center left; tc=top center; tcr=top center right;
tr=top right; cl=center left; c=center; cr=center right; bl=bottom left;
bcl=bottom center left; bc=bottom center; bcr=bottom center right;
br=bottom right; bg = background.

Photographs

40bl, 41tr, 46tr, 47bl, 50bl, 68bcr, 68-69tc, 72-73tc, 75bc, tl, 79cl, 81tc **Alamy;**
19cl, 35tl, 42c, 62b, 69cl, 78tr **Bridgeman Art Library;** 8bc, 9br, 11tr, 12tcr,
14c, 16tr, 17tcr, tr, 18bl, 19bc, 20c, cl, 22bc, 23br, 24bc, 25br, tr, 27c, tcr, 28bc,
cr, 29br, tc, tl, 30-31c, 32cr, 34br, 35bl, tcr, 36tr, 37cr, 39bc, 44cl, cr, 45br, 48c,
49tl, tr, 50-51tr, 51cr, 52c, tr, 53br, 55tl, 56tcl, 57bcl, bcr, tcr, 58cl, 58-59tc,
59br, 60bcl, br, 61br, 62-63tc, 64-65bl, 65bl, br, tl, 66-67bl, 71br, 74bc, cl,
76cr, tr, 77br, 78bc, br, 80bl, tr, 80-81c, 81br, cr, 82br, 84-85c, 85bc, c, tr, 87bl,
c, tc, tr, 89cr, tr, 92-93c, 93br **Corbis;** 8tr, 9cl, 10br, 14tcr, 20tc, 23tr, 32bl,
36-37c, 38c, 43tcl, 45cr, 46cl, 50tc, 51br, 63tr, 66bl, 70tr, 72bc, cl, 74tr, 76bl,
76-77tr, 78cl, 90cl **Getty Images;** 2br, c, 3tc, 10bcl, tr, 16-17bl, 17bc, c, 21br,
23tcl, 24tc, tr, 25tl, 26bc, tcr, 27bl, br, 28bl, 29bc, tc, tl, tr, 30cl, 31bc, c, tr,
33bl, 34cr, 37tc, 40tr, 41tl, 42-43bc, 43cr, 45tr, 48bc, br, 53c, tc, 55br, 56bcl,
58-59cr, 64tcr, 66tr, 67br, cr, tc, 68br, cl, 69cr, 71c, tc, 72bc, 73br, 77bl, cr,
82bl, 83tr, 84cl, 89bl, 90-91bc, 92bc, br, 94br, tc, 95bcl, bcr, bl, br, tcl, tl
iStockphoto.com; 10tcl, 34cl, 35br, 49bc, 62cr, 71bl **Lonely Planet;** 12bcr,
49br **The Picture Desk;** 2bl, 3bc, bl, br, 4c, 6bc, bl, cr, 6-7tc, 7bcr, bl, tcr, 9c,
tc, tr, 10c, tcr, 11tl, 12bl, 13tc, 15bc, br, tl, tr, 16cl, 18bcr, cl, tcr, tr, 19tr, 20-21c,
21cr, tr, 22tr, 23bl, 27tl, 28tr, 29bc, 30bl, 32c, cl, 33br, 34tr, 36cl, 37bl, tr, 38bc,
tr, 39tc, tl, tr, 41bcr, bl, c, 42bl, tc, 43tcr, tr, 44tr, 44-45c, 53cl, tr, 54tr, 54-55bl,
55cl, tr, 56-57c, 57bc, tc, tl, 58bc, 59bc, cl, tr, 60tcl, 61bc, tc, 62cl, 63bc, br, c,
tl, 64tl, 65tr, 66tr, 67cl, tl, 68c, cr, 69br, tc, 71tl, tr, 73bc, 74bcr, tcr, 76c, 77tr,
81tl, 83cr, tr, 84bl, tc, 85r, 86c, 87br, 88bl, tc, 88-89cl, 89tc, 91c, cl, tc, 92cl,
93bl, t, 94bc, bcr, bl, tcr, tr, 95bc, tc, tc **Shutterstock;** 13bcl, br, tcl, 15bl, cl,
17tl, 20bc, 39c, 46-47bc, 50c, 61bl, 82tr, 83br, 86bl, 86-87tc **Topfoto.**

All repeated frames and image motifs courtesy of iStockphoto.com

Illustrations

Cover illustrations by **Chris Corr.**

73tc **Paul Bachem;** 4-5c, 94bcl, 95tr **Chris Corr;** 70bc **Rob Davis/The
Art Agency;** 11bc, 32-33tr, 40c **Geri Ford/The Art Agency;** 72bl, 73tr
Tony Gibbons/Bernard Thornton Artists UK; 47cr **Dave Smith/The
Art Agency**

All illustrations and maps copyright 2012 Weldon Owen Publishing

LONELY PLANET OFFICES

Australia Head Office
Locked Bag 1, Footscray, Victoria 3011
Phone 03 8379 8000 Fax 03 8379 8111

USA
150 Linden St, Oakland, CA 94607
Phone 510 250 6400 Toll free 800 275 8555 Fax 510 893 8572

UK
Media Centre, 201 Wood Lane, London W12 7TQ
Phone 020 8433 1333 Fax 020 8702 0112

lonelyplanet.com/contact